Maria Koran

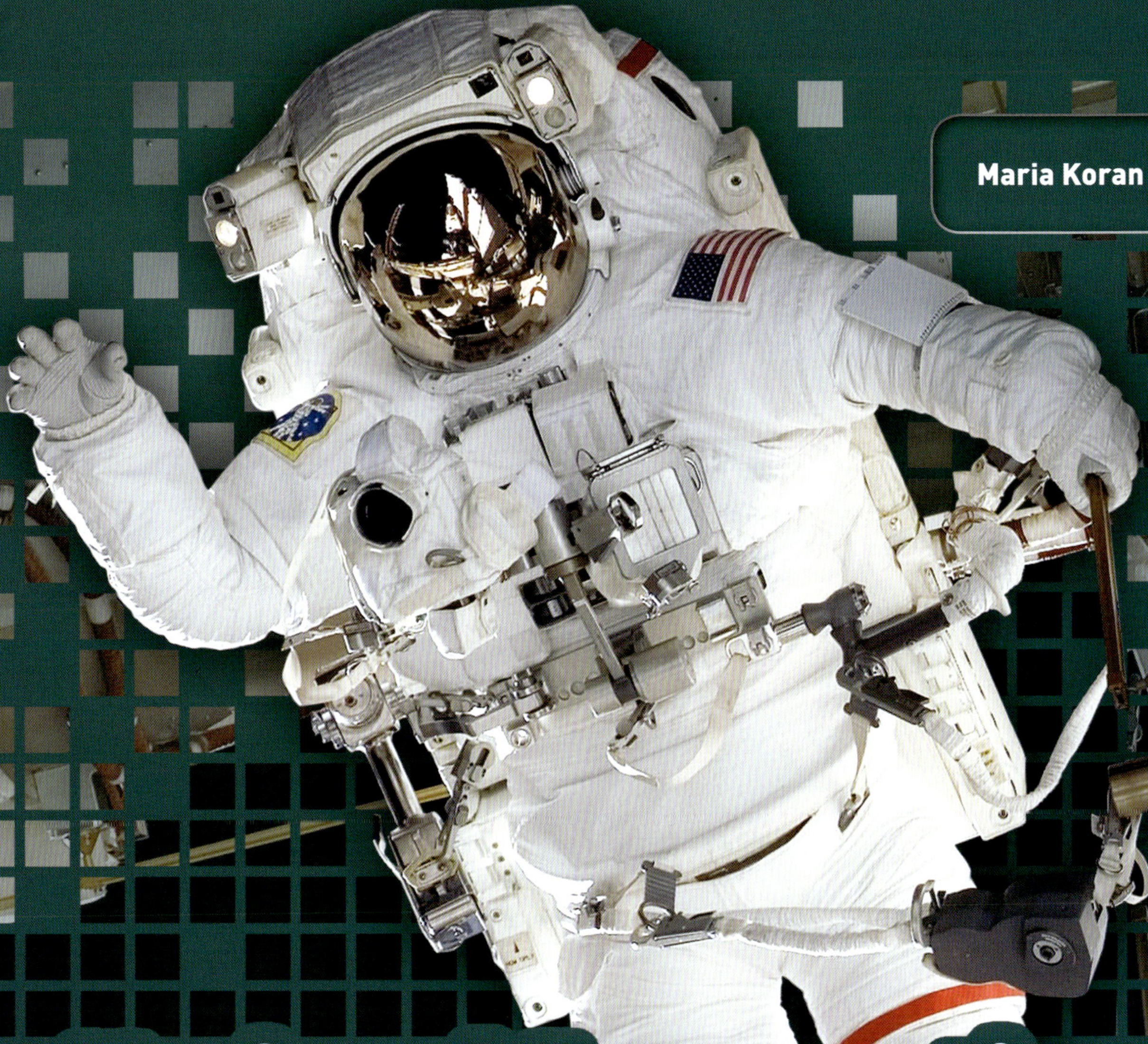

National Aeronautics and Space Administration

POWER • AUTHORITY • GOVERNANCE

LIGHTBOX
openlightbox.com

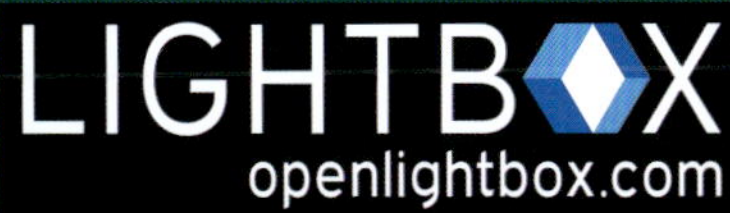

Go to
www.openlightbox.com
and enter this book's
unique code.

ACCESS CODE

LBXX7773

Lightbox is an all-inclusive digital solution for the teaching and learning of curriculum topics in an original, groundbreaking way. Lightbox is based on National Curriculum Standards.

STANDARD FEATURES OF LIGHTBOX

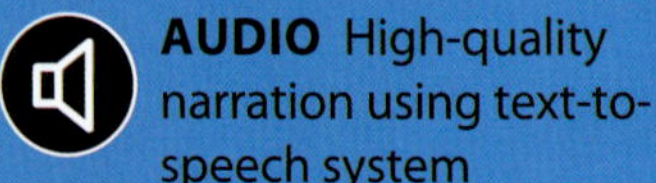
AUDIO High-quality narration using text-to-speech system

VIDEOS Embedded high-definition video clips

ACTIVITIES Printable PDFs that can be emailed and graded

WEBLINKS Curated links to external, child-safe resources

SLIDESHOWS Pictorial overviews of key concepts

TRANSPARENCIES Step-by-step layering of maps, diagrams, charts, and timelines

INTERACTIVE MAPS Interactive maps and aerial satellite imagery

QUIZZES Ten multiple choice questions that are automatically graded and emailed for teacher assessment

KEY WORDS Matching key concepts to their definitions

MORE Extra information and details on the subject

FIRST HAND Letters, diaries, and other primary sources

DOCS Speeches, newspaper articles, and other historical documents

POWER • AUTHORITY • GOVERNANCE

National Aeronautics and Space Administration

CONTENTS

Introduction

The National **Aeronautics** and Space Administration (NASA), was established in 1958. NASA is primarily focused on space exploration to help us better understand our **universe**. Since its establishment, NASA has had many missions attempting to uncover the mysteries of space. From the first moon landing in 1969 to today, NASA continues to be an integral part of humanity's understanding of space and our planet.

The Vehicle Assembly Building (VAB) at Kennedy Space Center is where NASA assembles its space vehicles. It is the largest single-story building in the world.

NASA is an independent agency of the United States federal government and is responsible for the country's space program. The space program includes civilian space flight programs, aeronautics, and aerospace research.

The U.S. government is based on the idea of **"popular sovereignty,"** meaning that U.S. citizens determine the nature of the government and its various parts. Therefore, even though NASA is an independent agency of the U.S. federal government, its purpose is scientific discovery and exploration for the benefit of the United States and its citizens.

135 space shuttle missions have been flown. **All launched** from the **Kennedy Space Center** in Florida.

Since **1992**, NASA's headquarters have been located at **300 E Street SW** in Washington, D.C.

NASA uses **"light years"** to describe distances in space. A light year is the distance light travels in one calendar year. One light-year is **6 trillion miles** (6,000,000,000,000 miles).

Origins of NASA

The origins of NASA go back to the Cold War. After World War II ended in the mid-20th century, a battle between the world's two greatest powers began. On one side was the **democratic** United States. On the other side was the communist **Soviet Union**. Although they were allies in World War II, the relationship between the two nations was a tense one. Each country was trying to outdo the other and, with the advancement of **nuclear** weaponry, a deadly arms race was underway.

Dwight Eisenhower was a five-star general in the U.S. Army prior to becoming president.

During this time, space exploration became a new frontier to establish technological, economic, and political superiority. Reaching these new heights would establish which nation was the most advanced. This competitive quest to explore space was known as the "space race." Soon, both nations would be exploring the stars.

On October 4, 1957, the Soviets launched *Sputnik*, the world's first artificial **satellite**. This became the first man-made object to be placed into the Earth's orbit. Soon after, in 1958, the United States launched its own satellite, *Explorer I*. That same year, President Dwight Eisenhower signed a public order creating NASA, a federal agency dedicated to space exploration.

Branches of Government

NASA is not a part of the Department of Defense. It is also not part of any **cabinet**-level department. NASA's administrator reports directly to the president of the United States.

As an independent agency of the United States Federal Government, NASA receives its funding from the annual federal budget passed by the United States **Congress**. Congress controls the budget of all NASA programs, including aeronautics research, robotic spaceflight, technology development, and the human space exploration programs.

Purpose of NASA

NASA provides the United States with a lot of information. Whether it is about the Earth, the **solar system**, or the universe, NASA is at the forefront of space exploration. For example, information from the NASA Earth Science program provides information about Earth that plays a vital role in the country's scientific advancement, national security, and even economy.

Sir Arthur Eddington was a British scientist. His 1919 experiments with starlight helped NASA researchers today understand how the universe works.

NASA's mission statement requires them "to pioneer the future in space exploration, scientific discovery and aeronautics research."

To complete their mission, NASA does not just shoot rockets into space. Although space exploration is certainly an important part of their job, they also conduct experiments on biology, chemistry, anatomy, and other areas of science, as they relate to space. For example, they study how the human body works when there is no gravity.

NASA used the space shuttles to help build the *International Space Station (ISS)*.

Although many people do not realize it, many of the things that NASA must invent to complete its missions become part of our daily lives. Artificial limbs, solar panels, and even smoke detectors had their beginning with a NASA invention.

As we learn more about the universe, the purpose of NASA continues to change and evolve.

The Freedom of Information Act

Created in 1966, the Freedom of Information Act (FOIA) provides that any person has a right to obtain access to federal agency records. This means that the FOIA allows public access to executive branch information in the federal government.

This allows any citizen of the United States to request information that not only NASA is recording, but also what any federal agency is recording. This Act ensures that citizens are informed, and it is vital to a democratic society.

NASA has designed its new programs so that the public has access to all mission documentation. This allows U.S. citizens to see exactly how NASA spends all of the money it is given by Congress.

NASA Through the Years

NASA was created more than 60 years ago. Since then, it has been involved in many major events in U.S. history. Today, NASA continues to explore Earth's solar system.

October 4, 1957

The Soviet Union launches the first artificial satellite, *Sputnik*.

July 29, 1958

President Eisenhower signs the National Aeronautics and Space Act, creating NASA.

February 20, 1962

John H. Glenn, Jr., becomes the first U.S. citizen to orbit the Earth.

July 20, 1969

American astronauts Neil Armstrong and Edwin "Buzz" Aldrin walk on the Moon.

April 11, 1970

An exploding oxygen tank on *Apollo 13* jeopardizes the mission. After many days of problem solving, NASA is finally able to bring the astronauts home safely.

1973

The United States ends its involvement in The Vietnam War. This war was another area of conflict between the United States and the Soviet Union during the Cold War.

July 20, 1976

The *Viking 1* unmanned spacecraft lands on Mars and completes its mission.

April 12, 1981

The first space shuttle, *Columbia*, is launched.

January 28, 1986

The space shuttle *Challenger* explodes 73 seconds after launch. All on board are killed.

1995

GPS-guided missiles are invented using technology first developed by NASA.

1998

The Hubble Space Telescope sends back the first pictures of a planet outside of our solar system.

February 1, 2003

The space shuttle *Columbia* disintegrates while reentering the atmosphere. All crew members are lost.

March 2, 2016

Astronaut Scott Kelly returns to Earth after spending a year on the *ISS*. The experiment tested the effects on the human body of being in space for long periods of time.

September 15, 2017

The *Cassini* spacecraft completes its 20-year mission of exploring Saturn and crashes into the planet.

NASA Issues

Like any government agency, NASA has its share of issues and problems. Many of these problems arise from the public not really understanding what NASA does. One of the main arguments against funding NASA is that it pulls money from other government programs here on Earth. It is difficult to justify a million-dollar rocket when we should also worry about how to feed all of the people in the United States.

The agency is often also accused of having projects run over budget. When a NASA program that costs millions of dollars is planned, going over budget by even ten percent can be an enormous amount of additional money spent.

Although each NASA mission teaches people more about science, building one rocket costs more than 50 million dollars.

In recent years, NASA has been working very hard to educate the public on what it does and how money is spent. There are now daily broadcasts from the *ISS* for children, tours of NASA facilities, and other exciting educational programs. Each of these initiatives helps show citizens how NASA uses their tax dollars.

The House Committee on Appropriations

Almost all of the budgets that are given to departments and agencies in the executive branch of government must be approved by the House Committee on Appropriations. This committee is the responsibility of the **House of Representatives**, part of the legislative branch.

The committee contains members from both of the political parties in the United States, Republicans and Democrats. The chairperson for the committee is chosen from the political party that has the most members in the House of Representatives at that time.

Like other agencies, NASA must appear before the committee and explain how it developed its budget, how much money it needs, and how it will be used. Because the budgets approved by the committee use U.S. tax dollars, NASA often has to explain to the members of Congress how NASA's mission benefits the citizens of the United States.

In 2019, the chairperson of the House Committee on Appropriations was Nita Lowey. She is a representative from the state of New York.

NASA

Key Figures in NASA

There are hundreds of astronauts, scientists, technicians, and others that have all contributed to discoveries made by NASA.

Neil Armstrong

Neil Armstrong (1930–2012) was the first person to walk on the moon. He was also a college professor, test pilot, and engineer. Armstrong received the Presidential Medal of Freedom in 1969 and the Congressional Space Medal of Honor in 1978.

Sally Ride

Sally Ride (1951–2012) was the first U.S. woman in space and a brilliant physicist. She helped deploy two satellites as part of her first space flight. Following her flights on the space shuttle *Challenger*, she worked on international arms control and returned to her **physics** research.

Guion Bluford

Guion Bluford (1942–) was the first African American in space. His first spaceflight was on board the space shuttle *Challenger* in 1983. He was an engineer and U.S. Air Force fighter pilot before taking part in four space shuttle flights.

First Person on the Moon

HISTORICAL CASE STUDY

Throughout the 1950s and 1960s, the United States was in a "space race" with the Soviet Union. The Soviet Union had won the race to get the first satellite into space when they launched *Sputnik* in 1957. The United States was determined after that to be the first country to have someone walk on the Moon.

On July 16, 1969, *Apollo 11* was launched with astronauts Neil Armstrong, Buzz Aldrin, and Michael Collins on board. After three days of travel, they entered the orbit of the Moon. Collins then kept the command module in orbit while Armstrong and Aldrin took the lunar module, the *Eagle*, to the Moon's surface.

On July 20, 1969, the *Eagle* landed on the surface of the Moon. The radio transmission from the astronauts back to NASA of "The *Eagle* has landed" is one of the most famous events in history.

Neil Armstrong became the first person to walk on the Moon when he left the lunar module on July 21, 1969, followed 19 minutes later by Buzz Aldrin.

After stepping out of the lunar module, Neil Armstrong said one of the best-known quotes in science, "That's one small step for man, one giant leap for mankind."

Careers in NASA

Astronaut

Astronauts are the most iconic NASA workers. These are the brave men and women that are willing to risk their lives to test the rockets, space shuttles, and space stations that NASA creates. In addition to being in fantastic physical shape, an astronaut must also have an extensive background in science and engineering.

Rocket Scientist

The rockets and satellites that NASA builds are scientific works of art. The amount of science and technology that goes into just one rocket requires enormous teams of brilliant scientists. To get a job like this, a scientist needs many years of schooling in areas including physics and engineering.

Public Relations Specialist

NASA depends on the funding from tax dollars and the approval of the U.S. public. Because of this, the public relations specialists are an important part of the NASA team. These are the individuals that are responsible for telling people what NASA missions are for, how the missions are going, and what was discovered on a mission. They are the public face of NASA.

Aerospace Engineer

Probably the most important part of any NASA mission is how to get the rocket to where it needs to go. Figuring out how a rocket flies in Earth's atmosphere and in the vacuum of space is the work of an aerospace engineer. These individuals are the NASA employees that figure out how to get astronauts to their destination and then safely back home.

NASA's budget in 2019 was **$21.5 billion** dollars. This budget must be approved by Congress and uses U.S. tax dollars.

The head of NASA is known as **the administrator**. The administrator is nominated by the president and then confirmed by the U.S. Senate. On **April 23, 2018**, Jim Bridenstine became the 13th NASA administrator.

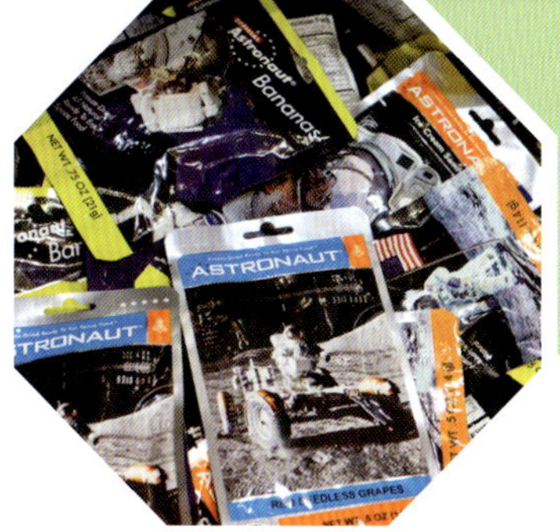

From making rockets to creating the food that astronauts eat, **nearly all** NASA jobs use at least one **STEM** field.

Tools of the Trade

NASA has many exciting and complicated tools that help it complete its mission. NASA is one of the international leaders in scientific development.

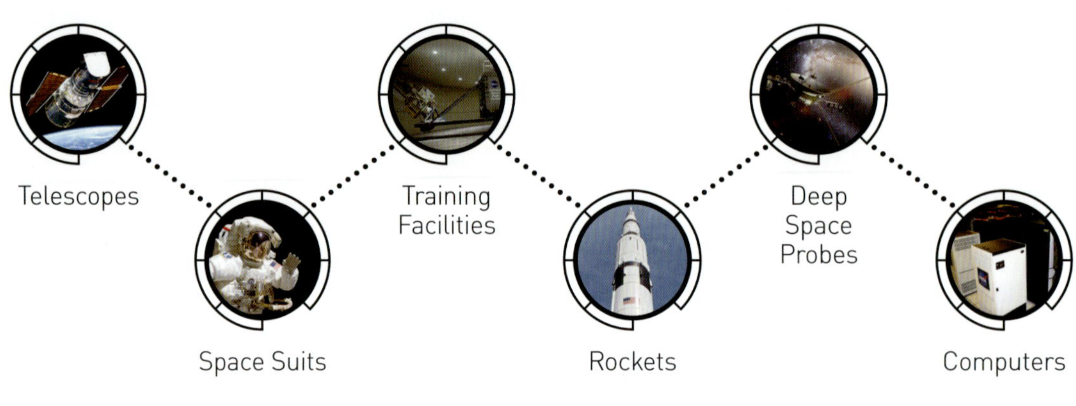

Telescopes

Since the earliest days of **astronomy**, telescopes have been important instruments for the study of space. NASA uses extremely powerful telescopes to help it learn more about space. Some of these telescopes are on Earth. Others, such as the Hubble Space Telescope, are out in space sending back pictures and information.

Space Suits

The space suits that astronauts wear are engineering marvels. These suits allow humans to live in the vacuum and frigid temperatures of space. They allow astronauts to breathe while walking on the Moon. The suits are designed to support all bodily functions as the astronauts perform their work.

Training Facilities

Space missions are extremely challenging physically. Astronauts must train to be able to handle the extreme pressures of liftoff, effects of zero gravity, and many other things. To help them, NASA has training facilities like underwater labs to simulate zero gravity and centrifuges to prepare them for liftoff.

Rockets

When NASA wants to get something into space, they use a rocket to do it. Rockets are the powerful machines that provide the huge force required to escape Earth's gravity. Once the satellite or other NASA device reaches space, it separates from the rocket and carries on its mission. The Saturn family of rockets have been used for many NASA missions.

Deep Space Probes

NASA is helping us to learn more about our universe every day. To do this, NASA has launched deep space probes that are designed to keep sending information for many years. These probes are solar powered and never meant to return to Earth. Their job is to keep going farther into space, sending back pictures and information.

Computers

NASA depends on computers. Computers help rockets get to where they need to go. They also help NASA handle the massive data from all their satellites. They even keep track of the health of the astronauts on missions. Some of the calculations that NASA must do are so complicated they do not use computers, they use **supercomputers**.

NASA in the United States

NASA has many different facilities across the United States. Some of these facilities are for research, and others launch rockets and satellites into space.

1

Los Angeles, California

The Jet Propulsion Laboratory (JPL) in Los Angeles is one the earliest NASA facilities. JPL helped with *Explorer 1*, the first satellite launched by the United States in 1958. One of the main jobs of JPL is to build robotic planetary spacecrafts. JPL also manages NASA's Deep Space Network.

2

Houston, Texas

The Lyndon B. Johnson Space Center (JSC) facility is responsible for training all of NASA's astronauts, as well as astronauts from other countries. JSC is also responsible for the United States Astronaut Corps. Because JSC is responsible for managing many of NASA's missions once they are underway, JSC is often referred to as "mission control."

CANA
UNITED STATES
MEX
Washington
Montana
Oregon
Idaho
Wyoming
Nevada
Utah
Colorado
California
1
Arizona
New Mexico
Pacific Ocean

LEGEND
Land (USA)
Land (Other)
Water

SCALE
400 MILES
700 KILOMETERS

3 Greenbelt, Maryland

The Goddard Space Flight Center (GSFC) is located in Greenbelt, Maryland. The scientists at GSFC build the equipment needed for space missions and manage missions. They are responsible for NASA's two communications networks, the Space Network and the Near Earth Network. They also work with the National Oceanic and Atmospheric Administration (NOAA).

4 Cape Canaveral, Florida

The John F. Kennedy Space Center (KSC) is probably the best-known NASA facility. KSC is responsible for the launch of every manned space flight since 1968. The Center's VAB is one of the largest buildings in the world. This is where all the pieces of a satellite or rocket are assembled before going into space.

NASA in the World

Although there is still competition between countries when it comes to space, scientists around the world have seen the advantage of working together. NASA and its international counterparts all work together to share discoveries and information.

The *ISS* is a research lab where scientists perform many different types of scientific experiments. Scientists from all over the world come to live and work on the station.

The *ISS* is probably the most well-known example of international cooperation. It was launched in 1998 and is a satellite that orbits the Earth. Astronauts and scientists from around the world live and work together on the satellite. The job of everyone on the station is to help us learn more about space.

The Canberra Deep Space Communication Complex is located in Australia. It is part of NASA's Deep Space Network.

International cooperation on space exploration also happens here on Earth. NASA works with other scientists at the telescope centers in Chile. They also work with the Canberra Deep Space Communication Complex (CDSCC) in Australia.

Probably the largest cooperation between international organizations is the sharing of scientific information and discoveries. Countries around the world no longer keep discoveries about space secret. As soon as a NASA scientist, or a scientist from another country, discovers something new about our universe, that information is made public.

Skylab was the **first space station** for the United States. It fell to Earth in 1979. People from all over the world were worried because no one knew where the pieces of *Skylab* were going to land.

Some NASA rocket flights **only have U.S. astronauts**. However, others carry **international** crews from **around the world**.

The Soviet Union, now Russia, launched and maintained the **Mir Space Station** from **1986–2001**.

NASA Today

It is an exciting time to be part of NASA. Missions to Mars and photographs of **black holes** are becoming a reality.

The recent missions to Mars have confirmed that our neighbor planet had water. This was a huge discovery since water is a basic need for life. In November 2018, the Mars lander *Insight* arrived on Mars and has since been sending back crystal clear images from the planet's surface. Every day we are learning more and more about the planet in our solar system that is most similar to Earth.

NASA is also revolutionizing our thinking about the universe from all of the pictures and data that are now being sent back from deep space probes. We are learning more about distant galaxies and objects in space that we had no idea existed. In March 2019, we even saw the first pictures of a black hole.

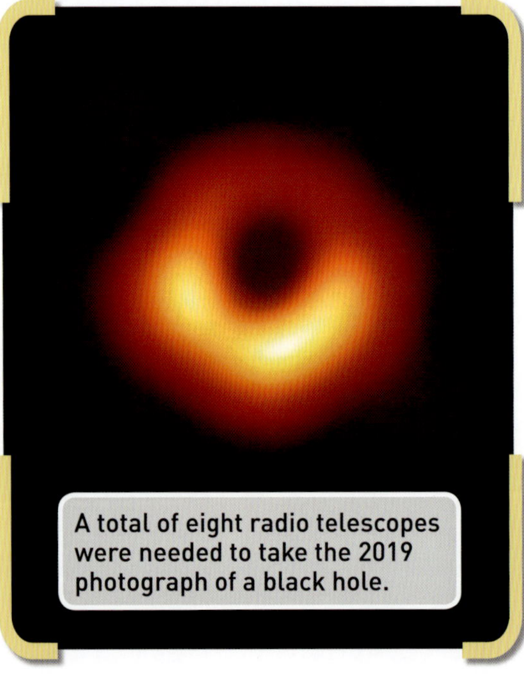

A total of eight radio telescopes were needed to take the 2019 photograph of a black hole.

Even given all of the fascinating discoveries that NASA is making, they still must do a better job of explaining to citizens of the United States, and to Congress, how these discoveries help mankind. For many citizens, it is difficult to justify millions of dollars just to see a distant galaxy while domestic programs that help people eat and have shelter also need funding.

The Cassini-Huygens Mission

MODERN CASE STUDY

On October 15, 1997, NASA launched the Cassini-Huygens mission to Saturn. The calculations involved were astounding. Given the years that it would take *Cassini* to get to Saturn, scientists had to launch it in the direction of where Saturn would be years from launch.

Cassini sent back pictures of Venus, Jupiter, and many other things during its flight, arriving in orbit on July 1, 2004. For the next 13 years in orbit, *Cassini* would send back pictures and information about the surface and rings of Saturn.

The *Cassini* spacecraft sent back detailed pictures that allowed scientists to discover two new rings around Saturn.

The Cassini-Huygens mission required thousands of scientists and engineers.

On December 25, 2004, the *Huygens* module that was attached to *Cassini* separated and landed on one of Saturn's moons, Titan. The module sent back data about Titan for 90 minutes.

Cassini ended its 20-year mission on September 15, 2017 when it entered Saturn's atmosphere and burned up.

NASA Looking to the Future

NASA has many plans and missions already in development. With new information and technology arriving daily, missions that would have been impossible in 1968 are now happening.

Using all of the information being sent back by the Mars lander, NASA is now planning a mission to Mars with actual astronauts. Although it will take years to get there once launched, we may actually have humans on the surface of another planet.

Mars landers allow NASA to view the planet's surface using tools such as high definition cameras.

Another exciting area of future research for NASA is the hunt for **"dark matter."** In the 21st century, scientists have come to believe that our universe is mostly made from a form of matter called "dark matter." This new type of matter is extremely difficult to detect, and NASA is one of the organizations trying to prove it exists. The space probes and other devices that NASA is inventing to find it are marvels of technology.

NASA will also be continuing with their research in deep space. We see stories in the news almost daily about some new, fantastic thing in space that we did not know existed. In the future, NASA will continue to teach us all about what exists in our universe.

ACTIVITY ★★

Create a Policy Paper

Although the missions from NASA teach us fantastic things about our universe, they are also extremely expensive. When distributing funds to government agencies from taxpayers, Congress must balance the need of the organization with the needs of the people.

Develop your own thoughts about how NASA should be funded and how much money they should get. Write a policy paper that summarizes your opinion.

Step 1:

Answer the following questions to help you develop your opinion.

1. Should NASA be funded with taxes from U.S. citizens? Why or why not?
2. Do you consider the missions from NASA important? Would you continue to fund NASA?
3. What government agencies do you think should receive more money than NASA? Why?
4. What needs of U.S. citizens should come before the need for more information about space?
5. Are there any types of NASA missions that you would not fund? Why?
6. How much money should NASA be given for shared, international missions like the *ISS*?
7. Should NASA be able to receive funds from anyone besides the U.S. government?

Step 2:

Take your opinions from Questions 1 – 7 and write a one-page policy paper. It should explain the policy you think is correct about how much money NASA should receive for its programs. It should also explain why.

- Paragraph 1: What is the problem?
- Paragraph 2: What different steps can solve the problem?
- Paragraph 3: Which step do you think should be taken? Why?

QUIZ

1 In what year was NASA founded?

2 What do the initials NASA stand for?

3 Which Act allows U.S. citizens to request information and records from the federal government?

4 Which U.S. president approved the creation of NASA?

5 Who was the first person to walk on the Moon?

6 What are three "tools of the trade" used by NASA?

7 What is the name of the space telescope that sent back pictures of a planet that is not in our solar system in 1998?

8 What committee in the House of Representatives reviews NASA's budget?

9 What planet was *Cassini* sent to explore?

10 NASA is part of which branch of the U.S. government?

ANSWERS

1. 1958 2. National Aeronautics and Space Administration 3. The Freedom of Information Act 4. President Harry Truman 5. Neil Armstrong 6. Telescopes, space suits, training facilities, rockets, deep space probes, computers 7. The Hubble Space Telescope 8. House Committee on Appropriations 9. Saturn 10. Executive

KEY WORDS

aeronautics: the science and study of flight-capable machines

astronomy: a natural science that studies celestial objects in the universe

black holes: regions in space with gravitational forces so strong nothing can escape from them, including light

cabinet: a group of people that advise the president of the United States

Congress: governing body of the legislative branch of government consisting of two chambers, the House of Representatives and the Senate

dark matter: a hypothetical form of matter that is thought to account for the majority of the matter in the universe

democratic: a system of government in which the people choose their leaders

House of Representatives: the lower chamber of the United States Congress

nuclear: relating to the nucleus of an atom

physics: the science and study of understanding how the universe behaves

popular sovereignty: the idea that the authority of a state and its government are controlled by the people of the state

satellite: an artificial or natural object that is in orbit

solar system: the Sun and everything in its gravitational pull including Earth and the other planets

Soviet Union: a socialist state in Eurasia that existed from 1922 to 1991

supercomputers: a computer with a high level of performance compared to a general-purpose computer

universe: the collection of all the things that exist in space

INDEX

SUPPLEMENTARY RESOURCES

Click on the plus icon found in the bottom left corner of each spread to open additional teacher resources.

- Download and print the book's quizzes and activities
- Access curriculum correlations
- Explore additional web applications that enhance the Lightbox experience

LIGHTBOX DIGITAL TITLES
Packed full of integrated media

VIDEOS

INTERACTIVE MAPS

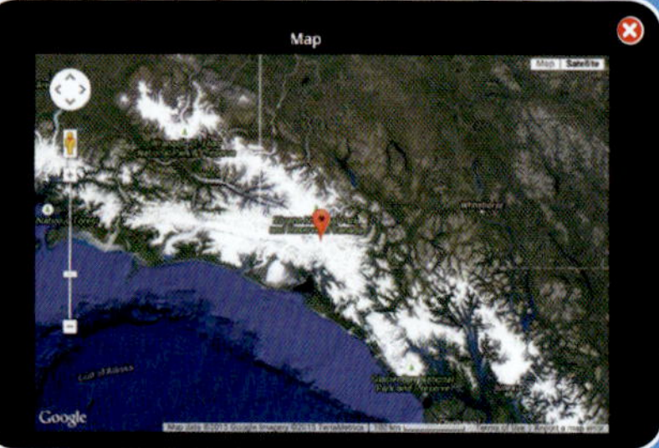

WEBLINKS

SLIDESHOWS

QUIZZES

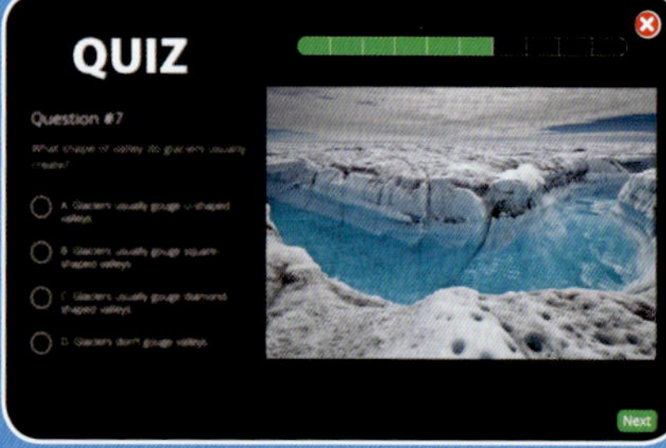

OPTIMIZED FOR

- ✓ TABLETS
- ✓ WHITEBOARDS
- ✓ COMPUTERS
- ✓ AND MUCH MORE!

Published by Smartbook Media Inc.
350 5th Avenue, 59th Floor New York, NY 10118
Website: www.openlightbox.com

Library of Congress Control Number: 2019939791

ISBN 978-1-5105-4673-8 (hardcover)
ISBN 978-1-5105-4674-5 (multi-user eBook)

Printed in Guangzhou, China
1 2 3 4 5 6 7 8 9 0 23 22 21 20 19

052019
122718

Editor: John Willis
Art Director: Terry Paulhus

Every reasonable effort has been made to trace ownership and to obtain permission to reprint copyright material. The publisher would be pleased to have any errors or omissions brought to its attention so that they may be corrected in subsequent printings.

The publisher acknowledges Alamy, Getty Images, Shutterstock, and Wikimedia Commons as its primary image suppliers for this title.